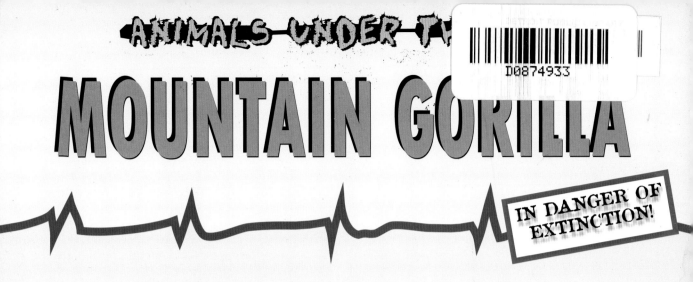

ANIMALS UNDER THE

MOUNTAIN GORILLA

IN DANGER OF EXTINCTION!

Marianne Taylor

Heinemann Library
Chicago, Illinois

NOV 0 4

KN

Design: Jo Hinton-Malivoire and Tokay,
    Bicester, UK (www.tokay.co.uk)
Picture Research: Rosie Garai and Liz Eddison
Originated by Ambassador Litho Ltd.
Printed in China by WKT
Company Limited

08 07 06 05 04
10 9 8 7 6 5 4 3 2 1

**Library of Congress Cataloging-in-Publication
Data**
Taylor, Marianne, 1972-
   Mountain gorilla / Marianne Taylor.
      p. cm. -- (Animals under threat)
Summary: Discusses the plight of mountain
gorillas and why they are near extinction,
as well as some of the ways humans can help.
Includes bibliographical references (p.   ).
   ISBN 1-4034-4861-2 (lib. bdg.), 1-4034-5435-3
(Pbk.)
   1. Gorilla--Juvenile literature. [1. Gorilla.
2. Endangered species.]
I. Title. II. Series.
QL737.P96T38 2004
599.884--dc22
                                2003016141

Acknowledgments
The author and publishers are grateful to the
following for permission to reproduce copyright
material:
pp. 4, 5, 7, 17, 34, 40 Digital Vision; pp. 6, 13
Adrian Warren/Ardea; pp. 8, 38 Andrew
Plumptre/OSF; p. 10 Gallo Images/Corbis/Gallo
Images; p. 11 Kennan Ward/Corbis; p. 12 P.
Ward/FLPA; pp. 14, 18, 30 Steve Bloom; p. 16, 24,
31 Martin Harvey/NHPA; p. 19 Michael
Leach/NHPA; p. 20 Mary Plage/Bruce Coleman;
p. 21 Martin Harvey/Corbis/Gallo Images; p. 22
Bruce Davidson/Nature Picture Library; p. 23 Karl
Ammann/Ecoscene; p. 25 Michael S. Lewis/Corbis;
p. 26 Corbis/Bettman; p. 27 Robert Maass/Corbis;
p. 28 Rex/Sipa; p. 29 Yaan Arthus-Bertrand/Corbis;
p. 32 Buddy Mays/Corbis; p. 35 Liba
Taylor/Corbis; p. 36 D. Parer & E. Parer-
Cook/Ardea; p. 37 Jeremy Williams/Rex; p. 42
The Dian Fossey Gorilla Fund; p. 43 Tudor
Photography.

Cover photograph reproduced with permission of
Corbis/Gallo Images/Martin Harvey.

Every effort has been made to contact copyright
holders of any material reproduced in this book.
Any omissions will be rectified in subsequent
printings if notice is given to the publisher.

The author would like to thank A, A, J, M and T.

Some words are shown in bold, **like
this.** You can find out what they mean
by lookingin the glossary.

Contents

The Mountain Gorilla

The mountain gorilla is the ultimate **great ape.** It is famous for its huge size and tremendous strength, but it is a peaceful, gentle animal. Mountain gorillas live quietly in the remote mountain forests of central Africa. They are the most famous, but also the rarest, kind of gorilla. There are so few of them left that they are in real danger of becoming **extinct** if they are not protected from the many threats they face.

Gorillas are the largest type of **ape** in the world. The other great apes are orangutans, chimpanzees, bonobos, and humans. The much smaller gibbons and siamangs are also apes. Apes belong to the group of **mammals** called **primates.** Monkeys, lemurs, and bushbabies are also primates. Of all the animals in the world, gorillas are one of the closest living relatives to humans. Ninety-eight percent of the gorilla's **genes** are the same as ours. All the large apes are rare and threatened with extinction, except for humans. We are the most common large mammals in the world, but our success has often been at the expense of other animals.

| gorilla | chimpanzee | orangutan | gibbon |

▲ *The great apes are the largest primates. They are all big, powerful animals, with large heads and no tails. The gibbon is a smaller type of ape.*

History and discovery of mountain gorillas

It is thought that many thousands of years ago, all gorillas in Africa were alike. Then, the forest they lived in became smaller and was broken up into separate, even smaller forests over hundreds of years. This caused the gorilla population to be split into three groups. The longer the three separate populations of gorillas remained apart from each other, the more different they became.

In 1902 Captain von Beringe, a German explorer, became the first European to see mountain gorillas. He was exploring what is now the country of Rwanda, in central Africa. Halfway up Mount Sabyinyo in the Virungas range, Beringe saw what he described as a "herd of big, black monkeys" climbing a hillside. His men shot and killed two of them. Beringe could not identify the animals. They were much bigger than the gorillas of the lowlands. He brought one of them back to the natural history museum in Berlin, where it was recognized as a new gorilla **subspecies.** The mountain gorilla, as it became known, was given the scientific name *Gorilla gorilla beringei*, in honor of Beringe.

▲ *The mountain gorilla is the largest, most powerful primate in the world.*

How many species of gorilla?

Until recently, people believed there was only one **species** of gorilla, divided into three subspecies. These were the eastern lowland gorilla, western lowland gorilla, and mountain gorilla. However, at the end of the 20th century new scientific methods of **genetic testing** were used to study these three kinds of gorilla. The results have suggested that the western lowland gorilla is probably genetically different enough from the other two to be treated as a separate species, which could not breed with the other two.

Gorilla Country

Mountain gorillas live in forests on the slopes of the Virunga mountain range. They are also found in the Bwindi Impenetrable National Park. It is located 20 miles (32 kilometers) north of the Virungas, in Uganda. The total area crosses the borders of three African countries: Rwanda, Uganda, and the Democratic Republic of the Congo (DRC). At their highest points these mountains are very cold, with very few plants. But lower down the slopes, there are various types of forests. The gorillas are found in the **montane cloud-forest** zone, at 9,840 to 11,480 feet (3,000 to 3,500 meters) above sea level. Here, the jungle is thick with vegetation. However, this is not a tropical forest. The temperature ranges from 45 to 68 °F (7 to 20 °C), and it often rains and hails.

*Although the forests lie close to the **equator**, they are so high up the mountain side that they are always cold and misty.*

A variety of wildlife

Gorilla habitat is good for all kinds of wildlife. The cloud forest has many kind of plants that support many **species** of animals. The gorillas share the forest with buffaloes, elephants, leopards, chimpanzees, and antelope. The forest also has several kinds of monkeys, other smaller **mammals** and around 300 species of birds.

The forest vegetation is very lush. Mountain gorillas can find plenty of plants to eat.

Forest food

Mountain gorillas are mainly **herbivores.** There is plenty of food for them in the forest, but some of the plants they need grow very slowly. After eating all the best pieces of vegetation in one place, a gorilla group will move to a new area of forest. This gives the vegetation a chance to grow back. Therefore, gorillas need to live in a much larger area of forest than they will actually be using at any one time.

One favorite food is bamboo shoots, which grow during the wettest times of the year. So the gorillas spend more time in the bamboo forest areas during the rainy seasons. Sometimes they go higher up into the mountain meadows about 13,120 feet (4000 meters) above sea level. There, the temperatures are below freezing at night, and there is less food for them. However, the giant senecio tree is found there. The soft center of its twigs is one of the mountain gorilla's favorite foods.

Habitat change

African forests are much smaller and more broken up than they were many years ago. Most of central Africa was covered in rain forest 5,000 to 7,000 years ago, and there were probably many more gorillas then. The **climate** has gradually become drier. Some of the forests have been replaced by other kinds of vegetation. In the 20th century, people cleared large areas of the remaining forest to use the wood and to create new farmland. The area of good mountain gorilla **habitat** that remains is so small that it cannot support many gorillas.

Gorilla Populations

The mountain gorillas' two areas of **habitat** are small and isolated. The gorillas do not move away from these areas. Researchers have carefully studied both areas for many years, and the gorilla population has been monitored very closely. A great deal is known about the way gorillas use their habitat, and about how much space each group needs. Also, there is so much research going on that many of the groups are seen and counted often. This means that the estimates of the total population are probably quite accurate. The most recent surveys of mountain gorilla numbers suggest that the total population is about 670.

The total population is divided into two main groups. About 355 mountain gorillas live in the Virunga range. The area they live in falls in three countries. Each country protects its gorilla area as a **national park.** The national parks are Parc National des Volcans in Rwanda; Mgahinga Gorilla National Park, in Uganda; and Virunga National Park, in the DRC. A separate population of about 292 is found in southwest Uganda, about 20 miles (32 kilometers) north of the Virungas, in the Bwindi National Park. Some scientists believe that the gorillas found here are a distinct **subspecies** called the Bwindi Gorilla, *Gorilla gorilla bwindi.*

Gorillas always stay within the forest areas and will not cross into the farmland that comes right to the forest edge.

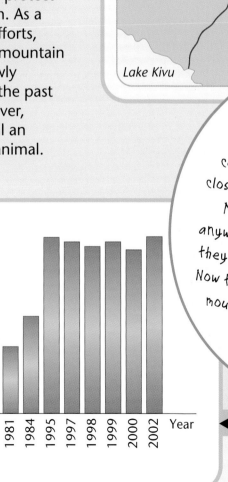

The mountain gorilla is found in two tiny areas of forest in central Africa.

Close to the edge

At the beginning of the 1980s, **extinction** seemed certain for the mountain gorilla. There were only about 250 in existence. **Conservationists** have worked hard to protect them since then. As a result of their efforts, the number of mountain gorillas has slowly increased over the past 20 years. However, the gorilla is still an **endangered** animal.

Bwindi National Park

Uganda

DRC (formerly known as Zaire)

Mgahinga Gorilla National Park

Virunga National Park

Parc National des Volcans

Rwanda

Lake Kivu

So few gorillas, so many people

Without very strict and careful conservation, we could lose one of our closest relatives from the world for good. Mountain gorillas have never lived anywhere other than central Africa, and they may never have been very common. Now they are extremely rare. For every mountain gorilla in the world there are more than nine million human beings.

This chart shows how the population of mountain gorillas has changed over the past 50 years.

Population

700
600
500
400
300
200
100
0

late 1950s
1973
1981
1984
1995
1997
1998
1999
2000
2002
Year

The Body of a Gorilla

Mountain gorillas are powerfully built animals. They have broad shoulders; long, muscular arms; and short, sturdy legs. They have strong, compact bodies with big, round bellies. Their necks are short and thick, and they have big heads with strong jaws and thick skulls. Their great size and bulk means that very few animals ever hunt and kill them. Having a big, chunky body helps them to keep warm in the mountain forests, which become very cold at night.

Males and females

Male mountain gorillas weigh about 350 pounds (160 kilograms), on average. They can be up to 6 feet (1.8 meters) tall when they stand up. Females are much smaller. They weigh between 154 and 250 pounds (70 and 114 kilograms), and are rarely more than (4 feet 1.2 meters) tall. In addition to being bigger than females, males have large, sharp **canine teeth.** These teeth are not used for eating. They are used in **displays** of strength and **aggression** between male gorillas. Usually, just the sight of a big male gorilla standing up and baring his huge teeth, while slapping his massive chest, is enough to keep another gorilla from attacking. Actual fighting is rare, but if they have to, gorillas will use their teeth and can inflict a severe bite.

An adult male gorilla shows his huge canine teeth.

The gorilla's life span

Mountain gorillas can live a long time. Their natural life span is probably 40 to 50 years. However, only about half of them survive to be adults. Once they are adults, the natural dangers they face, such as disease or accidental injury, are not nearly as serious as the dangers posed by the activities of humans.

Wrapped up warm

The fur of mountain gorillas is long, thick, and silky. It is usually dark brown to blackish-gray. It covers most of the body, except for the middle of the face, palms of the hands, soles of the feet, and a patch on their chests. The mountain gorillas' fur is much longer than that of lowland gorillas, which do not have to cope with cold temperatures. The hair on the backs of males becomes silvery-white as they grow older. Adult male gorillas are called **silverbacks.**

Getting around

Young mountain gorillas enjoy climbing and playing in the trees, but adults prefer to stay on the ground. They can climb if they need to, if they stick to branches strong enough to hold them up. However, there is plenty of food close to the ground, so this is where they spend most of their time. Mountain gorillas can stand up on two legs and walk on them for a short time. But their long arms and short legs make it easier to move on all fours, walking on their feet and hands.

When gorillas walk on all fours, they curl their hands into fists, so they are actually walking on their knuckles. They leave four knuckle prints in the ground.

Gorilla Lifestyle

The mountain gorilla's life is a pleasant one. The gorillas are sociable animals, spending most of their lives as members of a fairly stable group. There is usually very little conflict among the members of the group. The forest has plenty of the plants they like to eat, and they have little need to worry about being attacked by other animals. A **silverback** gorilla will fearlessly defend his group if danger threatens. But since no natural **predator** would try to take on a huge adult male mountain gorilla, gorilla groups are usually left alone.

Gorillas are not very lively. They spend most of their time resting. Only the young gorillas play energetically together. The adults prefer to lie around, sleep, feed, and groom each other. They usually feed for several hours in the morning and again in the afternoon. They take a long nap in the middle of the day. They regularly travel around the forest to find new feeding grounds. But they move at a slow pace. They travel less than a third of a mile (half a kilometer) per day. These animals are very laid-back.

▲ *Young gorillas are more active and more adventurous than adults.*

Mountain gorillas are well protected from the cold and rain of the forest by their long fur.

Sleeping arrangements

Gorillas are diurnal, which means they are awake during the day and sleep at night. Each night they build simple nests to sleep in. Sleeping in a nest helps to keep out the chill of the night. The nests are made out of plants and are built in tree branches or on the ground. Small babies share a nest with their mothers. Adults and **weaned juvenile** build their own nests. Gorillas learn how to construct a nest at an early age and become good at it. Usually the nest building takes only a few minutes.

What's on the menu?

The food supply of the gorillas is all around them. They rarely climb trees to **forage,** although they are very good climbers in trees that can hold them up. The big bellies of the gorillas contain long digestive systems to handle their vegetable diet. It is made up mostly of the roots, leaves, and stems of plants. The gorillas' large intestines are roughly twice the size of human intestines. A male adult gorilla eats up to 66 pounds (30 kilograms) of plants in a day. Gorillas occasionally eat **invertebrates,** such as beetle larvae and ants. But, unlike the closely-related chimpanzee, they never hunt other **mammals.**

Fur care

Gorillas are very clean animals. They groom their own fur every day. They also groom one another's fur, removing any skin **parasites** they find. This mutual grooming is a good way to keep the fur in good condition and to scratch those hard-to-reach places. The close, trusting contact also helps to start and keep friendships between individual gorillas.

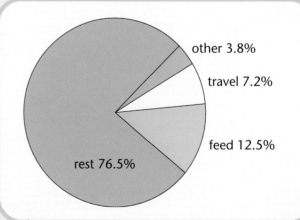

other 3.8%

travel 7.2%

feed 12.5%

rest 76.5%

This circle graph shows how mountain gorillas spend their time.

Gorilla Groups

Most mountain gorilla groups have only one adult male or **silverback,** sometimes known as the **alpha male,** and two or more adult females. The rest of the group is made up of their offspring— babies and **juveniles** of various ages and both sexes. The alpha male is the dominant member of the group. He decides what the group does and where it goes. He is bigger and stronger than all the others, and they rarely try to fight him. He is usually the father of all the young gorillas in the group. Among the adult females, the one who was first to join the group will usually be dominant over the one who arrived next, and so on. However, when females have babies, their rank may improve.

The usual group size is between 7 and 14 animals. Sometimes much larger groups form, with 30 or more members. Big groups might

A typical mountain gorilla group, with one adult male, several adult females and several juveniles of both sexes.

include two or more silverbacks, because it is hard for one silverback to be in charge of so many gorillas. However, when there are two or more silverbacks, one is dominant over the others. Larger groups seem to be less stable and often break up into smaller groups.

When it is time to leave the group

Males leave the group they were born into when they are around eleven years old. They then live alone. They cannot join an established group because the alpha male will drive them away. They must wait until they find their first female and can start a new group. They usually do not start a group until they are at least fifteen years old so they spend at least four years living alone. One out of every ten mountain gorillas is a solitary male. They have not yet acquired a **harem,** or group of females.

Females leave the group they were born into and move directly to a new group when they are around eight years old. They then begin to breed. They might join a lone male and start a new group. Females often choose to do this, rather than join an established group and be a lower-ranking female.

The young challengers

Sometimes one solitary young male will try to take over an established group. The alpha male of that group will usually be able to drive him away with **aggressive displays.** However, if the gorillas are closely matched in strength, they may fight fiercely. If the newcomer defeats the alpha male and takes over the group, he will often then attack and kill all the young gorillas in the group. It is thought that this will make the females ready to breed again very quickly. The new male will not have to spend time looking after the older male's offspring, but will start fathering babies of his own so he can pass on his **genes.**

Communication

Because they spend almost all of their lives as members of a group, it is important for gorillas to get along with one another. There is very little conflict among group members. They do not normally have to compete with one another for things such as food and mating opportunities. The **silverback** is in charge of the group, followed by the most dominant adult female and then the other adult females. The larger **juveniles** are dominant over smaller, younger ones. If any fights threaten to break out among the females or juveniles, the silverback will end the conflict with **displays** of **aggression** toward those involved.

Gorilla voices

Gorillas are far quieter than their cousins the chimpanzees, who make shrill, shrieking cries. However, they do communicate with sound. Their voices are low-pitched. The sounds they make are usually soft, perhaps because they usually are not more than a few yards (meters) away from one another. Researchers have so far identified around 20 different sounds that gorillas make. They include a variety of grunts, howls, hoots, and barks. Gorillas also beat their chests with cupped hands. Chest beating is a display of dominance, that is most often performed by the **alpha male.**

Dominant gorillas often get groomed by those of a lower rank.

No territories, large home ranges

Gorilla groups do not have **territories.** This means that they do not live in one specific area that they defend from other gorillas. Instead, they move about freely within the entire forest. So that the plants they eat can regrow, groups must regularly travel to new feeding grounds. Although gorillas move around a lot, they do not wander at random. They stay within a particular large area, or home range, that is usually several square miles (kilometers). They sometimes encounter other groups or solitary males on their travels. When this happens, the males will show aggression by chest beating, growling and teeth baring, and they may even fight physically.

How clever are gorillas?

Like other **apes,** gorillas are very intelligent animals. In studies, captive western lowland gorillas have been taught sign language, and they have used the signs to form simple sentences. They are able to ask for food or drink and describe objects in terms of their size and color. Some people think that they can also express abstract ideas. For example, they will "talk" about objects that are not with them at the time. We do not know whether wild gorillas use anything that could be described as a language. Even after years of study, people cannot yet speak "gorilla." They cannot completely understand what gorillas say to one another with their sounds and gestures. But the sign language studies suggest that they may be able to communicate with one another at a quite complex level.

Play is an important way of learning social behaviors.

Female gorillas are mature at about 8 years old and start **breeding** at about 10 years. Males are usually in their mid-teens before they have attracted their first female and have their first opportunity to breed.

This male and female are courting.

Courtship

For a few days each month, a female gorilla goes into estrus. This means she is ready to mate and become pregnant. At this time, she will approach the **silverback** of her group. She stares at him with her lips pursed and may follow him around or reach out to him. After she has gained his attention, the two will mate. The silverback mates with all the females in his group when they go into estrus. Gorilla courtship is simple because their groups are very stable and usually have only one adult male. In some other **primates,** such as chimpanzees, the breeding system is very different. Females choose mates from several available males, so males have to compete with each other to impress the females. This makes courtship a more important part of their lives.

Pregnancy and birth

A female gorilla's pregnancy lasts eight and a half months. Then, a single baby is born, or sometimes twins. It usually takes only a few minutes for the baby to be born. The mother usually will not become pregnant again until her baby is about four years old, so she has a long time to devote to the care of each baby. This is important, because baby gorillas grow slowly and have a lot to learn from their mothers. Usually, gorillas are devoted mothers who take great care of their babies.

Gorilla mothers have a baby once every four or five years.

Gorillas and women

A lot of old legends about gorillas, both in Africa and elsewhere, suggest that male gorillas will grab human females if they get a chance. In some African cultures, women will not go on their own to areas where gorillas are found, in case they are chased by a lovelorn silverback. In the famous film *King Kong*, the giant gorilla King Kong falls in love with a human female. He seizes her and runs away with her. In truth, an adult silverback will have a **harem** of several female gorillas, all of whom seem more interested in him than he is in them!

A newborn mountain gorilla baby is completely dependent on its mother for her milk and her protection from danger. She keeps the baby close to her at all times, holding it against her chest. A baby gorilla has stronger hands, arms, and legs than a human baby, so it can cling tightly to its mother's body. It will not fall off if she needs to use both hands to climb, provided she moves carefully.

Caring for the baby

New mother gorillas know something about caring for a baby from watching other females. However, first babies often do not survive, sometimes because the mother does not have experience. She has to learn to keep her baby very close and not to leave it on its own, when **predators** might take it. She must also be careful not to let the other gorillas too close to the baby while it is still very small. Sometimes, other members of the group will injure or kill a baby gorilla in their eagerness to play with it. As mothers gain experience, the survival rate of their babies improves.

Baby gorillas are very appealing. Unfortunately this makes them targets for poachers, who try to capture and sell them.

Baby snatchers

Baby gorillas are lively bundles of black fluff. They have round faces and wide eyes, without the frowning expression of adult gorillas. Their charming appearance and delightful character make them desirable animals for people who keep zoos. They are also much easier to handle than full-grown gorillas, which can overpower people. Animal traders will pay a lot of money for gorilla babies so **poachers** often try to capture them to sell to traders.

The early years

A very young baby clings to its mother's chest all the time. After a few months, it will begin to ride on her back. By the time it is a year old, the baby is beginning to eat solid plant food. However, it keeps drinking milk from its mother until it is about three years old. The baby slowly learns from its mother and the other gorillas in the group which foods are best and how to find them.

Becoming independent

As they grow bigger and stronger, young gorillas spend more time away from their mothers and begin to play with other youngsters in the trees. By the time they are five, they can **forage** by themselves, and their mothers will usually be caring for the next new baby. The young gorillas spend about three more years with the group they were born in. They grow bigger and stronger and learn about the forest and how to be a gorilla. They learn a great deal through play. When they finally leave to join another group or start a new group, they have all the skills they need to survive.

Up here, a baby gorilla is safe from danger and gets a good view of its world.

Conflict Between Gorillas and Humans

Long ago, mountain gorillas had very little to fear from other animals. The only large **predator** that shares their **habitat** is the leopard. But even this strong big cat would not take on a **silverback** gorilla that is defending his group. There have been a few cases of leopards attacking lone female or **juvenile** mountain gorillas, but this is very unusual. However, human beings with guns or spears can kill adult mountain gorillas, and they have been doing so for many years.

Hunting for meat

Mountain gorillas have been hunted for meat for many years, but not in large numbers. Many populations of wild animals are not harmed by small-scale hunting. But there are so few mountain gorillas that even occasional hunting is now a serious problem. Eating gorilla meat is **taboo** for the local people. But in hard times that taboo will be broken. Gorillas can also be accidentally caught in **snares** set by hunters to catch other animals, such as antelope.

Some people have always found the idea of hunting big, powerful animals exciting. However, this attitude is far less common today than it was 100 years ago.

Poaching

In more recent times, gorillas have been hunted for other reasons besides food. There are people who sell or collect items made from the body parts of wild animals, including gorillas. Unbelievably, a garbage can made from an elephant's foot or an ashtray made from a dead gorilla's hand are considered attractive and valuable trophies by some people. There is a market for gorilla heads, feet, and hands. The rarity and size of mountain gorillas mean that their body parts are especially valuable and prices for them are very high. Killing animals when it is against to law to do so is called **poaching.** The gorillas' habitat is protected and killing gorillas is illegal, but that does not always stop the poachers because they can make a lot of money this way.

▲ Workers will attempt to return this rescued baby to the wild.

Killed for the cure?

Many kinds of animals are killed by poachers, and their body parts are sold to make traditional medicines. The larger, rarer, and more spectacular the animal, the more it is wanted. In traditional medicine, powdered tiger bone is believed to cure many illnesses. Some African cultures use medicines that come from gorillas.

Taken alive

There are also people willing to pay thousands, or even hundreds of thousands of dollars for living mountain gorillas to keep in zoos and private animal collections. Poachers try to catch baby gorillas alive. But gorilla mothers keep their babies close to them, and all the gorillas will fight fiercely if their group is attacked. Therefore, the hunters will usually have to kill some adult gorillas in order to capture a baby.

Destroying Gorilla Habitats

As people have increased in number, developed more sophisticated tools, and spread throughout the world, they have made many changes to most types of natural **habitat.**

The gorillas' habitat is totally destroyed by forest clearance.

Forests are of little use to people as a place to live in or cultivate. But the trees supply wood, which is extremely useful. As the trees are cut down, the cleared land can be used for farming or other kinds of **development.** The wood from some of the trees that grow in the Virungas is quite valuable, and some of it is sold to other countries. It is also used locally as firewood. **Logging** has recently taken place in the mountain gorilla forests, although they are supposed to be protected. In 1969 the trees in almost half the area of the Parc National des Volcans were cut down to create new farmland.

Slow to grow

Ancient forest takes a long time to regrow. The biggest trees may be several hundred years old. Forests planted by people for wood production tend to contain fast-growing tree **species,** that are ready to be cut down in just a few decades. They support far fewer animals than the rich, varied natural forests. It is not possible to quickly replace the habitat that the gorillas have lost.

The need for farmland

In the countries where mountain gorillas live, the human population is growing all the time. These people need to eat, and they need land on which to plant crops and graze their domestic animals. The governments of the countries want to protect their unique wildlife, but they need to help people develop farmland. There is a lot of pressure on the remaining **cloud forest.** To the desperately hungry people, the forest may look like wasted land that could be used to grow food. In 1983 the government of Rwanda seriously considered allowing a 12,000 acres (4,856 hectares) of the Parc National des Volcans to be cleared for agriculture. Meanwhile, local people enter the forest and cut firewood or graze their **livestock** there. The forest is continually being eaten away.

As their habitat shrinks, the gorillas are beginning to find it more difficult to find food. There are a few reports of gorillas **foraging** among farmers' pea and corn fields. This creates more conflict between the gorillas and the local people.

These terraces make it possible to farm on very steep slopes. This can lead to encroachment onto gorilla **territory.**

Carl Akeley was a gorilla hunter who later supported their conservation.

The explorer Carl Akeley was the first to strongly campaign for the **conservation** of mountain gorillas and their **habitat.** In 1921 he went on a mission to the Virunga Mountains to collect mountain gorilla specimens for the American Museum of Natural History. He and his party killed several gorillas. But when Akeley examined a dead **silverback,** he had a sudden change of heart. He was struck by the gorillas' humanlike appearance, and he began to feel that it was wrong to kill animals that were so like humans. He had also come to realize how rare the animals were. He approached the Belgian government, which controlled that area of Africa at the time, and suggested that the mountain gorillas should be protected, not killed.

National parks

Due to the efforts of Akeley and others, Albert National Park was established by the Belgian government on April 21, 1925, to protect its mountain gorillas. It was the first **national park** to be established in Africa. On July 9, 1929, the boundaries of the park were extended to include almost the entire Virunga volcano chain. The area remains officially protected land, even though the boundaries and governments of the countries it falls in have changed several times. Today, the Virunga forest spreads across three countries. Rwanda, Uganda, and the **DRC** each protect their own area of the forest as a national park. It is an island of wild habitat in the middle of densely populated farmed land.

The other mountain gorilla area, Bwindi Impenetrable National Park in Uganda, first became a Forest Reserve in 1932. Its trees were protected, and any cutting down of trees was strictly controlled. At this time, the protected area was at the center of a much larger area of unprotected forest. By the end of the 1980s, the unprotected forest areas had all been cut down. The remaining area, the Forest Reserve, was declared a national park in 1991. Study of the gorillas in Bwindi National Park has been going on ever since.

George Schaller

Biologist George Schaller came to the park in 1959 to carry out the first serious field study of mountain gorillas. Assisted by his wife Kay, he spent a year working with the gorillas. The animals became **habituated** to them and after a while accepted their close presence. George Schaller was able to record details of mountain gorilla behavior that had never been seen before. He wrote a book, *The Year of the Gorilla*, which is still extremely useful for researchers studying these animals. The knowledge the Schallers gained about the gorillas and their way of life has since helped conservationists decide how best to protect the animals and their habitat.

George Schaller carried out the first detailed study of mountain gorilla behavior.

Dian Fossey

Dian Fossey was the most famous mountain gorilla researcher. She was born in California in 1932 and grew up with a great love of animals and wildlife. She saw her first mountain gorillas when she was on vacation in Zaire (the country now known as the **DRC**) in 1963. She was enthralled by the magnificent animals.

Appendicitis?

The anthropologist Dr. Louis Leakey met Fossey on her first trip to Zaire in 1963. In 1966, he met her again in Louisville, Kentucky, and asked if she would like to work for him studying mountain gorillas. Fossey jumped at the chance. Leakey said she needed to have her appendix removed before she could return to Zaire, because the operation could not be carried out there if she happened to need it. She had the operation, but then discovered that it was not necessary at all—Leakey was just testing her determination to work with the gorillas!

Getting closer

Fossey began studying gorillas in Zaire in 1966. After a few months she moved to Parc National des Volcans in Rwanda, where she established a new camp called Karisoke. She spent many years at this camp studying the gorillas. By quietly imitating their behavior, she gained their trust. Soon, she could sit close to them without alarming them. In 1970, she became the first person to have friendly contact with a wild mountain gorilla when a young adult male called Peanuts approached her and touched her hand.

Dian Fossey gradually earned the trust of wild mountain gorillas.

The gorillas' champion

Fossey was a tireless worker for gorilla **conservation.** She created extra patrols of guards and instructed them to capture any **poachers** they found. She worked to prevent cattle grazing inside the park. She also fiercely resisted the attempts of the Rwandan government to allow gorilla tourism.

In 1977 poachers killed her favorite gorilla, a **silverback** known as Digit. Fossey was grief-stricken, and became even more determined to protect the gorillas she considered to be her friends. Some said that she became dangerously obsessed with finding and punishing poachers. She eventually made many enemies in Rwanda through her determined and uncompromising views. One of these enemies turned out to be deadly. On December 26, 1985, Dian Fossey was found murdered in her cabin. To this day it is not known who killed her.

A lasting legacy

Fossey's contribution to mountain gorilla conservation was huge. The Digit Fund, started by Fossey in 1978, is now known as the Dian Fossey Gorilla Fund International. It continues to raise money, fund research, and run the Karisoke Research Center. Other organizations have since been started, such as The Mountain Gorilla Conservation Fund. Fossey's book, *Gorillas in the Mist*, and the film based on it, have done much to raise public awareness of the mountain gorillas' situation.

Gorilla Tourism

By the 1980s, the mountain gorillas of the Virungas were one of the best-known populations of wild **mammals** in the world. The problems of **habitat** loss, hunting, and **poaching** were also well understood. It was clear that the gorillas were very seriously threatened with **extinction.** It was vital to protect them and their habitat. The cost of providing this protection is huge, and new ways to make money were needed.

Ecotourism is small-scale tourism. It involves local people, has a low impact on the environment, and uses the money raised to help fund **conservation.** In the 1980s, the Rwandan government began to organize gorilla-watching tours to raise money. The idea was not supported by everyone involved in gorilla conservation, but it quickly became a very useful source of income for the country. It helped fund the protection of the park. Ecotourism made the gorillas more valuable to Rwanda in their own right, as living animals. The other gorilla parks also began to host gorilla tours.

*Watched by local children, gorilla-watchers set off for the forest at the Parc des Virunga, **DRC.***

Fame and fortune

Far from Africa mountain gorillas were becoming movie stars. In 1988 the film, *Gorillas in the Mist*, about the life of Dian Fossey was released and became a box-office hit.

People in many countries had already seen mountain gorillas on television in the ground-breaking natural history series *Life on Earth* (first screened in 1979). British natural history broadcaster David Attenborough sat among a group of mountain gorillas. The animals played gently with him, completely relaxed in his presence. All this led to an increase in tourism, because people wanted to go out and see these wonderful creatures for themselves.

Is it harmful?

Some researchers are concerned that gorilla tourism may not always be good for the animals. It is a good way of making money, but the welfare of the gorillas must come first. Some tours get too close to gorillas or bring groups of 30 or more tourists. Tourism has become very popular, but more research into its effects on gorillas must be done. Some scientists say that gorilla tourism should be more strictly controlled than it is at present.

Tourists who are lucky enough to see these animals in the wild are unlikely to forget the experience.

Visiting the relatives

In the Virungas, ten **habituated** gorilla groups are used for tourist visits. Tourists, in groups of 6 to 8, can watch the gorillas from as close as 16 feet (5 meters) for up to an hour. The park guards are with them at all times, making sure they do not get too close to the gorillas or disturb them in any way. Tourists who have been on these tours describe the experience as magical.

Gorillas in Contact with Humans

If not for researchers like Dian Fossey and others who followed her, people's knowledge of a mountain gorilla's way of life would be much less complete. Fossey and others **habituated** mountain gorillas to the close presence of humans. There would also be very little chance of creating a successful **ecotourism** industry based around seeing mountain gorillas. However, this habituation comes at a price.

Captive lowland gorillas, like this one, are gentle with their keepers and visitors.

Infectious diseases

Gorillas can catch many of the diseases that affect humans. However, the outbreak of an **infectious disease** could be much worse for them. They would have no natural **immunity** to it because they have never been exposed to it before. There are cases of captive lowland gorillas catching measles from humans. The wild population of mountain gorillas is so small that any infectious disease could be a disaster for them. If a tourist has an illness, he or she is not allowed to approach the gorillas.

Too close for comfort?

Another possible problem with habituation is that the gorillas could become too trusting of humans and lose their natural cautiousness around people. This could increase the risk of groups being attacked by **poachers.** It is also possible that the close human contact is stressful and harmful to the gorillas in ways scientists do not yet understand. One well-watched group in the Bwindi National Park lost seven of its original ten members at the end of the 1990s, and no one is sure why this happened.

There is also the possible risk of the gorillas harming their human visitors. Gorillas are certainly powerful enough to harm or injure humans. There are no recorded fatal attacks, but some researchers have been on the receiving end of **aggressive** displays from **silverbacks.** A couple of times a researcher has been charged at and knocked down. It is important never to surprise the gorillas, block their path, reach for them, or do anything that might seem threatening to them. Respectful and intelligent behavior from visitors and researchers is necessary at all times.

Peaceful gorillas

When they do not feel threatened, gorillas pose no danger to humans. The rewarding experiences of Dian Fossey and many others who have spent time with mountain gorilla groups show how gentle they really are. This seems to be true of all kinds of gorillas, not just the habituated mountain gorillas of the Virungas. On two occasions children have fallen into lowland gorilla enclosures at zoos, injuring themselves in the process. Onlookers were horrified and expected the worst. But in both cases the gorillas treated the injured children with great care and gentleness, standing guard over them until they were taken away by zookeepers.

The countries in which mountain gorillas live have long histories of conflict. There is an ongoing struggle between two tribes, the Hutus and the Tutsis, for control of the area. This conflict recently erupted into one of the most terrible wars of the 20th century. The war began in 1990, when rebel forces invaded Rwanda from neighboring Uganda. They planned to overthrow the Rwandan government. Although another four years were to pass before the war reached its height, the effect of the invasion on Rwanda's tourism industry was immediate. No one wanted to risk being caught up in a war for the sake of seeing mountain gorillas.

Several gorillas were killed by soldiers during the war, including silverbacks trying to defend their groups.

In the firing line

Hundreds of thousands of people died in the war. It was not surprising that the researchers and park keepers could do little to keep the mountain gorillas safe in the midst of such a large-scale human tragedy. A popular **habituated silverback** known as Mrithi was an early gorilla casualty. On May 21, 1992, soldiers shot and killed him after surprising him and his group. The rest of the group escaped. But their future group structure was bound to be upset by the loss of their leader. At least fourteen more gorillas have been killed during the war. Many were killed by **poachers** who took full advantage of the situation. It became too dangerous for any gorilla workers to remain in the area. In 1994 the camp at Karisoke was closed.

The gorillas' *habitat* lay in the middle of the war zone. This refugee camp was in the DRC.

Refugees

Between 1990 and 1994, about a million Rwandan refugees fled to camps at the edge of the Virungas. It is estimated that while in the area, these refugees cut down around 36 million trees for firewood. Soldiers planted thousands of land mines in the forest. This endangered both gorillas and researchers.

The consequences of war

The conflict has died down in recent years, but fighting still breaks out here and there. Karisoke was reopened in 1999, and the researchers were able to resume their studies. The gorilla tourism industry will take longer to recover. In 1999 eight tourists were killed in Uganda after they were abducted by Rwandan rebels. The warden (guard) of the Bwindi National Park and three of his rangers were killed trying to protect the tourists. More recently, three tourists were abducted by members of the same rebel group, and they have not been heard from since.

The situation in Rwanda has had very serious results for the local people and for the gorillas. The pressure on the governments to make the land available to people for farming has increased even more. As long as the area remains so unstable, protecting the animals and the forest is a big challenge. Trying to develop gorilla tourism is also a problem.

Although the mountain gorilla has been officially protected for nearly 100 years, it is still a seriously **endangered** animal. Its small population, limited **habitat,** and slow **breeding** rate means it will be in danger of **extinction** for many years. The continued problems of habitat loss, hunting, **poaching,** and human conflict could still spell the end for the mountain gorilla.

Almost all the world's mountain gorillas live in the four official **national parks.** These areas are carefully guarded to try to keep the gorillas safe and to keep people from cutting down the trees or grazing their **livestock** in the park. The job of being a park guard is difficult and dangerous. The guards require a lot of training, and they expect a good salary. They are on the front line of gorilla **conservation.**

Ongoing research into the lives of mountain gorillas is important for conservation.

Legal protection

The mountain gorilla has strict legal protection. It is listed in Appendix 1 by CITES (pronounced sightease), the Convention on International Trade in Endangered Species of Wild Fauna and Flora. This is an hagreement signed by 161 nations to control and regulate trade in wildlife, especially **endangered** wildlife. Nations can impose harsh penalties on people found guilty of poaching Appendix 1 animals. It is hoped that this will stop poachers. But the more difficult it is to get hold of mountain gorilla body parts, the more money collectors are willing to pay for them. So some poachers will still take the risk.

Justice

On January 30, 2003, three poachers were imprisoned for four years and fined about $8,200 for killing gorillas in Rwanda. In May 2002 they had killed an adult female gorilla in order to steal her baby, and another adult female who had tried to protect the baby. The baby gorilla was rescued, and the Dian Fossey Gorilla Fund is attempting to return it to the wild.

Raising money is essential for gorilla research and protection. Model Rachel Hunter is seen here at a Born Free Foundation fundraising party in 2002.

Research and fundraising

Research helps scientists decide how best to protect the gorillas and the forest. The Mountain Gorilla Geomatics Project began in 1992. It concentrates on monitoring the gorillas' movements and activities within the forest. The results of these surveys are analyzed alongside maps of the forest's plant types. Then, scientists can work out how best to manage the habitat for the benefit of gorillas.

Research and guard patrols are expensive, so fundraising is important. The Dian Fossey Gorilla Fund is one of several organizations active in raising money for the conservation program. Other wildlife **charities** make contributions. Besides directly funding conservation, the money is used to support the local community. This is an important part of gorilla conservation. If local people are doing well, they will not be a threat to the gorillas. Money can buy textbooks for children, pay for water tanks to be installed, and create credit funds to support the farmers living next to the forest.

Will Mountain Gorillas Always be Threatened?

When closely related animals breed together, their offspring are more likely to have health problems.

Thanks to the dedicated work of **conservationists,** the mountain gorilla population has increased in the last fifteen years. However, there are still fewer than 1,000 mountain gorillas living today. They reproduce at a very slow rate, and only half of all babies survive to **breeding** age. Therefore, it will take a long time for mountain gorilla numbers to increase further.

Captive breeding

Some **endangered** animals have been saved from **extinction** through captive breeding. Wild animals are caught and bred in captivity, where the babies can be completely protected from all danger. When they are old enough, the babies are released into the wild. This works well for some animals, but not for gorillas. Many of a gorilla's survival skills are learned rather than **instinctive.** If it grows up away from its natural habitat, it will not know how to find food and avoid danger.

The shrinking forest

Another problem that could keep gorilla numbers down is a shortage of proper **habitat.** The forest they live in is completely surrounded by farmland, and it has become smaller and smaller over the years. There is room in the forest for more gorillas than there are at the moment, but it is very unlikely that mountain gorillas will ever live anywhere other than in the Virungas. It may be possible to increase the size of the forest by planting new trees, but it will take hundreds of years for them to grow big enough to form good habitat for the gorillas.

Genetic problems

Another problem the mountain gorillas could face is one that can affect any very small animal population. In small, isolated populations, the animals often have very similar **genes** to one another, because no new animals ever arrive to breed with the rest and add new genes to the **gene pool.** If a disease spreads through the group and all gorillas share a low resistance to it, they might all die. Some scientists think that gorillas from the Virungas should be moved to Bwindi, or from Biwindi to the Virungas, so that the gene pool is enlarged, giving some group members better resistance to disease.

A special animal

The mountain gorilla was probably a rare animal even before human activity put it in real danger. Today it is even rarer, but it is also one of the world's best-known and most familiar animals. Its magnificent appearance, impressive size, and startling similarity to humans make it one of the most fascinating animals in the world. While this is the reason that **poachers** are so determined to hunt it, it is also why so many people are prepared to spend a great deal of time and money to protect it.

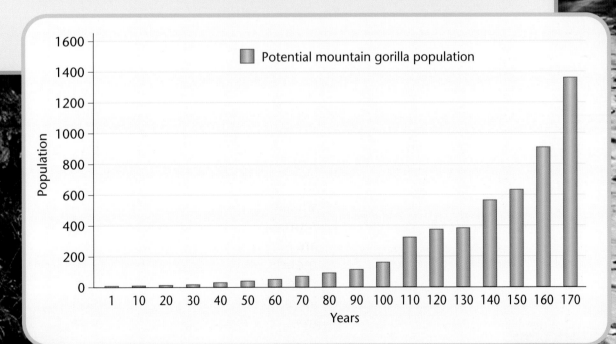

In theory, this is the rate at which mountain gorilla numbers would increase if there was no human interference.

The Future for Mountain Gorillas

It is hard to imagine a time in the future when mountain gorillas and their **habitat** will not need careful protection. **Poachers** are determined to hunt them, and their small habitat is constantly threatened with destruction. Political problems in the countries they live in could easily disrupt the whole **conservation** operation again. However, there are many dedicated people, both local and from abroad, who are willing to work tirelessly to keep the gorillas from becoming **extinct.**

*Mountain gorillas, the gentle giants of the wild **cloud forest,** are one of the real treasures of the natural world.*

Reasons to be hopeful

Mountain gorilla numbers are slowly continuing to increase. By sheer luck, the direct impact of the war on their numbers was not too serious. The **national parks** are now as well protected as they were before war broke out. The gorilla tourism industry is slowly recovering from the effect of the war. And the Rwandan government is working hard to build and maintain political stability and to attract more tourists. These efforts are bringing in more money, all of which is good for Rwanda and good for the gorillas.

Keeping up the good work

The ongoing work of researchers at Karisoke and other camps is also important to help protect the gorillas. There is still a lot to learn about gorilla behavior and lifestyle. The effect of tourism on the gorillas is one important area for future research.

Returning to the wild

Often it is difficult to reunite rescued gorilla babies with their groups. In 1991 attempts were made to return a rescued two-and-a-half-year-old to her group. Unfortunately, the group rejected her and she had to be recaptured. Another young female called Mvuyekure was rescued from poachers in October 2002. She was to be released in January 2003, but sadly she died before the attempt could be made. Despite many disappointments, researchers will continue to try to return any rescued young gorillas to their groups. With so few mountain gorillas left in the world, every single animal needs to have the best possible chance of living and **breeding** in the wild.

If the mountain gorilla is to survive, the forest must be protected from further destruction and the gorillas themselves must be protected from poachers. The best way to do this is to make sure that gorilla conservation goes hand-in-hand with programs that support the local people.

Many wildlife **charities** collect donations to help with mountain gorilla **conservation.** The Dian Fossey Gorilla Fund is probably the most active. One of their popular fundraisers is Adopt a Gorilla. For a donation of between $40 and $400 you receive an adoption certificate, a photograph of your gorilla or gorillas, and a T-shirt. This makes an unusual gift and is a fun way to help gorillas.

There are lots of ways you can raise money for gorilla charities, such as sponsored activities or a school rummage sale. Maybe you could sponsor your teacher to dress in a gorilla costume for a day!

Join in and speak up

Another way to support gorilla conservation, while learning more about it, is to become a member of a wildlife organization. For a small annual fee you will usually get regular magazines or newsletters telling you about the organization's work. It may organize events you can attend. It may also help you to make a difference, such as by telling you how to write to your representative in Congress. He or she has a duty to listen to your concerns, as well as the power to speak up about important issues in Congress. Wealthy countries can do a great deal to help poorer countries with their conservation concerns.

Digit, the gorilla whose death led Dian Fossey to form the first mountain gorilla fundraising organization.

Support Africa and the forests

Encourage your family to check that whenever they buy household objects made of wood, the wood has a label saying that it has come from a **sustainable** source. Excessive **logging** has ruined many of the world's **rain forests** and put all forest animals at risk of **extinction.**

Get muddy!

Learn more about the work of the gorilla conservationists and maybe even try some conservation work yourself. Working in conservation can be very tough, but it is extremely rewarding. There will always be a need for workers to monitor and study **endangered** animals.

If you are interested in practical conservation work, you could join a local wildlife group and get involved in projects like pond digging, tree planting, and counting wild animals. Developing skills such as these is excellent preparation if one day you decide you would like to work with gorillas or other endangered animals.

▲
Writing letters is a way of bringing the mountain gorilla's plight to the attention of those who can make a difference.

aggression showing willingness to attack another animal

agriculture using land to grow crops or to graze domestic animals

alpha male dominant male gorilla in a group

apes types of primates that do not have tails

breed produce babies

canine tooth long, pointed tooth or fang

charity organization set up to help others

climate general pattern of weather in a particular area

cloud forest forest that is so high above sea level that it is in the clouds

conservation protecting wild animals and their habitats from destructive forces. A conservationist is someone who works in conservation.

development change that is supposed to improve land or habitat

display activity performed by an animal that has a particular message. Chest beating by gorillas signals aggression.

DRC Democratic Republic of the Congo, a country in central Africa. It was formally known as Zaire.

ecotourism kind of tourism that benefits habitats, wildlife, and local people

endangered in danger of dying out

equator imaginary line around the middle of the earth, that divides it into northern and southern halves

extinction no longer living

forage   search for food

gene pool   all the genes of a group of animals, that are in contact with each other and breed together

genes   part of a cell that controls how an organism looks and how it will survive, grow, and change through its life

genetic testing   looking at an animal's genes in the laboratory, to see how closely related it is to other animals

great apes   group that includes chimpanzees, bonobos, orangutans, humans, and gorillas

habitat   place in the natural world where a particular organism lives

habituate   get a wild animal used to humans, so that it will behave normally even when humans are nearby

harem   group of female animals who are all the partners of one male

herbivore   animal that eats plants

immunity   resistance to disease. An animal or person with an immunity to an infectious disease will not catch that disease from any other animal or person.

infectious disease   disease that one animal can catch from another

instinctive   knowing how to do something without having to learn it

invertebrate   animal without a backbone

juvenile   young animal

livestock   animals kept for meat or milk, or to be sold

logging   cutting down of trees. Loggers are the people who carry this out.

mammal warm-blooded animal with hair and a backbone that can feed its young with milk from its body

montane environment that is found on the slopes of mountains

national park area of natural beauty protected by law

parasite tiny animal that lives on or inside another animal's body.

poaching catching or killing an animal illegally. A person who does this is called a poacher.

predator animal that hunts, kills, and eats other animals

primates group of mammals including lemurs, bushbabies, monkeys and apes

rain forest ancient, mature forest found close to the equator, that has very heavy rainfall.

silverback older, adult male gorilla

snare trap to catch a wild animal

species group of living things that are similar and can reproduce together to produce healthy offspring

subspecies group within a species that can breed with all members of that species

sustainable way of farming or logging that can be carried out without permanently harming or changing the land it uses

taboo activity that people avoid, because they believe it is wrong, unhealthy, or will bring bad luck

territory particular area an animal claims as its own and defends from others

weaned when an animal no longer takes milk from its mother

Useful Contacts and Further Reading

Conservation Groups and websites

The Dian Fossey Gorilla Fund International
www.gorillafund.org

The Mountain Gorilla Geomatics project
www.informatics.org/gorilla/gorilla.html

WWF
www.panda.org

National Geographic magazine
www.nationalgeographic.com/kids/creature_feature/0007/gorillas.html
This is an interesting feature all about mountain gorillas.

Books

Naden, Corinne J. and Rose Blue. *Dian Fossey: At Home With the Giant Gorillas.* Brookfield, Conn.: Millbrook Press, 2002.

Wood, Richard and Sarah. *Dian Fossey.* Chicago: Heinemann Library, 2001.

This book is written for teenagers and adults, but you might want to try reading it:

Fossey, Dian. *Gorillas in the Mist.* Houghton Mifflin Company, 1983.

Index